# WORDS THAT SELL

## SELL

### THE THESAURUS TO HELP YOU PROMOTE YOUR PRODUCTS, SERVICES, AND IDEAS

RICHARD BAYAN

CONTEMPORARY BOOKS

**Library of Congress Cataloging-in-Publication Data**

Bayan, Richard.
  Words that sell.
    Reprint. Originally published: Westbury, N.Y.:
Caddylak Pub., c1984.
    Bibliography: p.
    Includes index.
    1. Advertising copy.    2. Vocabulary.    I. Title.
  [HF825.B35    1987]    659.1'014    86-29319
  ISBN 0-8092-4799-2

*This book is dedicated to my parents*

This edition published by arrangement with Asher-Gallant Press, a division of
Caddylak Systems, Inc.


Published by Contemporary Books
A division of The McGraw-Hill Companies
4255 West Touhy Avenue, Lincolnwood (Chicago), Illinois 60712-1975 U.S.A.
Copyright © 1984 by Caddylak Systems, Inc.
Printed in the United States of America
International Standard Book Number: 0-8092-4799-2

    02  03  04  05  06  BAN  39  38  37  36  35  34  33  32  31  30  29 ˙28  27  26  25

# Table of Contents

# Preface

Like magicians with their props, or fishermen with their time-tested lures, advertising copywriters rely upon a handy assortment of contrivances for seducing an audience. A copywriter's tools are words, and the most effective tools are words that *sell*. Infallible adjectives like *superb* and *irresistible*. Ageless phrases like *a lifetime of satisfaction* and *right at your fingertips*. And, of course, that sturdy old standard, *FREE*!

This volume represents an attempt to gather the most potent of these words and phrases into a single sourcebook. To compile this material I rummaged through mountainous stacks of magazines, newspapers, brochures, and catalogs. I kept an ear open for compelling phrases heard over the radio and television. I raided my own copy files, consulted more than one thesaurus, and, after organizing the entries into lists, added still more words and phrases as they came to mind. I rejected those entries that seemed to fall flat in print, and shunned any slogans closely identified with specific products.

Think of this book as your personal magic kit—or, if you prefer, a bottomless tackle box filled with glittering lures. Use it whenever you require inspiration on short notice. Browse through its lists at leisure to expand your repertoire. With this book at your side, you'll be able to go straight to the words and phrases that suit your needs. Instead of groping for words, your mind will be free to focus on the real task of promotion: shaping a message that generates an enthusiastic response from your audience.

# Acknowledgments

During my formative years as a copywriter, I thought it might be a wise idea
to compile a notebook of words and
phrases to help me in my work. I toyed
with the notion and let it pass.

Then a strange thing happened. Some-
body offered to *pay* me for compiling
such a notebook. Motivated by the pros-
pect of fame and riches, I set to work,
filled a boxful of note cards, and produced this book (which I still plan to use
in my work).

I would like to thank the people who
helped bring this project to fruition: Ed
Werz, for having the vision to publish
a book so much more ambitious in
scope than my original idea; Ginny
Christensen, my friend and catalyst, who
(as usual) knew how to get things done;
and Judy Makover, my editor, whose
patience and wisdom are a continual
source of inspiration. I would be remiss if
I did not also acknowledge those name-
less writers of advertisements, brochures, catalogs, and sales letters, whose
collective opus furnished me with so
much of my raw material.

# How to Use This Book

At some time in your life you've probably used a thesaurus—a reference book filled with lists of synonyms. This book is a thesaurus of words and phrases used in advertising and other promotional writing.

As in any standard thesaurus, the entries in this volume are organized by topic. Look up **Stylish**, for example, and you'll find terms like *elegant* and *smashing*. Under **Convenient** you'll encounter *easily adjustable* and *take it anywhere*, among others. But look again: this thesaurus departs from the usual format in several respects.

- This book is organized into sections that correspond with the natural progression of sales literature from beginning to end.

  **1. GRABBERS**—the heads, slogans, opening statements, and provocative questions that catch the reader's attention.

  **2. DESCRIPTIONS AND BENEFITS**—the words and phrases used in body copy to convey the qualities of your product or service.

  **3. CLINCHERS**—the closing statements that can push an undecided reader over the response threshold.

  **4. TERMS AND OFFERS**—the "bottom line" that can make or break an advertisement.

The fifth section, **SPECIAL STRATEGIES**, provides you with lists of aggressive phrases for specialized purposes—from **Flattering the Reader** to **Knocking the Competition**.

- Each section is in turn subdivided into topics. If you want to expand upon the idea of "big," for instance, go to the section **DESCRIPTIONS AND BENEFITS** and find the topic **Big/Many**, which provides you with a list of words and phrases conveying that concept. If you're looking for an intriguing question with which to lead off your copy, turn to the section **GRABBERS** and find the topic entitled **Opening with a Question**.

The Table of Contents gives you a complete listing of sections and topics. If the topic you have in mind is not listed there, you will probably be able to find it in the Key Word Index at the back of the book. In fact, you might find it more convenient to check the index first, then refer to the appropriate list.

*Note:* In **DESCRIPTIONS AND BENEFITS**—by far the longest section of the book—the topics are arranged alphabetically for quick reference.

- The words and phrases supplied for each topic are not necessarily synonymous—they're simply useful expressions gathered in one place to help you express the idea you have in mind. Under **Sensory Qualities**, for example, you'll encounter words as disparate as *spicy* and *windswept*. Yet you'll probably notice that similar expressions tend to clump together within a given list.

• Many of the phrases contain blanks or trail off in an ellipsis (...) where the phrase breaks off. For example:

> The first _____ to address the problem of...

Here you've been supplied with the *pattern* for a phrase, which you can easily adapt to your needs by filling in the missing words or extending the phrase as you see fit.

Some further words of advice: for best results, familiarize yourself with the format of the book. Once you do so, you'll find that the arrangement by "natural progression" is a real convenience.

This book does not pretend to be exhaustive. I fully expect, in the coming months and years, to stumble across words and phrases that would have made first-rate entries. No doubt you will, too. When you find them, why not write them down under the appropriate topic and expand the collection. In time, my book will become *your* book—and that's the way it was meant to be.

*Note:* We invite you to participate in the next edition of *Words That Sell*. If you discover any additional words or phrases that belong in this book, send them to Caddylak Publishing, 201 Montrose Road, Westbury, New York 11590.

# A Copywriting Primer

The copywriter uses words as tools to persuade and motivate an audience. You *persuade* your readers that you have something valuable to offer; you *motivate* them to acquire it for themselves. This is the essence of effective copywriting—whether you opt for the hard sell or the subliminal suggestion.

The following guidelines, distilled from my own experience as well as that of other professional copywriters, should help you avoid some of the hobgoblins to which members of our tribe too often fall prey. At the same time—and with a minimum of trial and error—you'll gain the perspective you need to start writing "words that sell."

## Before You Write

1. *Analyze your product or service.* Do a little research to get your facts straight. Assemble your data from current sources of information (marketing reports, evaluations, product managers, existing copy); then, for best results, examine the product first-hand from a consumer's point of view. Define the nature of the product and enumerate all the features that would be of interest to a prospective consumer.

2. *"Position" your product or service.* How is it different from or superior to the competition? What do you offer that the competition doesn't? Positioning is critical if you want to develop a successful marketing strategy in a competitive situation.

3. *Assess your audience.* Always gear your copy to the needs and tastes of your readers. Are they everyday consumers? Upscale young professionals? Hard-boiled buyers with a bottom-line mentality? Executives in your field? Find out by checking the demographics of the media in which you'll be advertising, or (in the case of direct mail) by obtaining a breakdown of your mailing lists.

4. *Plan your attack.* Decide how much copy will be necessary to convey the message. (As a rule of thumb, the length of your copy should vary in direct proportion to your company's investment in the product. But not always. If your product is simple and its virtues self-evident, you don't have much explaining to do.) Other points worth considering: Do you want to develop a focal point or a running theme? Do you want to advertise a line of related products? And be sure to coordinate your plans with the designer so that you're both working with the same concept in mind.

## When You Write

1. *Don't lose sight of your primary goal: to sell your product or service.* Your writing should be more than a flat presentation of the facts. (Remember that a copywriter must persuade and motivate.)

On the other hand, don't let runaway creativity bury the message. The most brilliant efforts will be wasted if your audience can't remember your company's name. Write to sell.

2. *Don't fill your copy with empty over-statements.* Too many words like *fabulous* and *extraordinary* within a brief space will destroy your credibility. You don't want your audience to dismiss you as a propagandist. Instead, try to *convince* the audience that your product is fabulous. Make *them* say, "That's really extraordinary!"

3. *Be accurate.* Be sure you get the facts straight. Don't leave yourself open to claims of false advertising by making statements that can't be substantiated. Above all, be *truthful.* Resist the temptation to distort the facts for an easy sale. (Your sins will find you out, anyway.)

4. *Be specific.* Don't use vaporous abstractions or vague approximations when you have a chance to create vivid images with simple, observable details. Would you rather eat a "frozen dessert" or a "raspberry ice"? And try to avoid the notorious "than what?" comparisons: for example, "lasts longer" (than what?) or "gets the job done faster" (than what?).

5. *Be organized.* Your message should progress logically and inexorably from the headline to the clincher. Don't bury essential information in the darkest recesses of your copy or lead off with trivia that stops the reader cold. Like an old-fashioned short story, your copy should have a beginning, a middle, and an end.

6. *Write for easy reading.* Your style should suit the audience you're addressing, but certain rules apply to *all* copy. Cultivate a style that flows smoothly and rapidly, a style that's clear, uncluttered, involving and persuasive. Avoid long, convoluted sentence constructions. Affect a crisp but friendly and extraverted tone. *Communicate.* You want to do everything possible to insure that your message gets read.

7. *Don't offend.* Humor is a controversial issue among advertising insiders. A good many experts preach against it, but there's no denying that humor can be an effective tool—if it suits the subject or situation. (You don't want to joke about insurance or funerals.) Sarcasm, cynicism and other extreme forms of individuality are not likely to meet with mass approval. Don't criticize your audience's taste in clothes, music, pets, or anything else. Don't preach. Be of sunny disposition, and aim to please.

8. *Revise and edit your work.* Cut out all dead wood; every word should pull its weight. (Copywriting is like poetry in this respect.) Be your own critic. Check your facts, your syntax, your spelling. Make sure you haven't left anything out.

# PART 1
## GRABBERS

Making the Reader Sit Up and Take Notice

# Heads and Slogans

Switch to _____

Success starts with _____

The _____ that works as hard as you do

It's time for _____

_____ spoken here!

_____ means business

How do you turn a _____ into a _____?

The legend lives

Some straight talk about _____

_____ doesn't have to be expensive

_____ fever!

A little _____ can go a long way

Get comfortable with _____

Break away from the pack with _____

Not just another _____

Your partner in _____

Why your first _____ should be a _____

The _____ advantage

The _____ edge

A _____ for all seasons

Taste the difference!

Only _____ gives you...

Seeing is believing

The best-kept secret in _____

For the finest in _____, look to _____

They don't call us _____ for nothing

Always go to an expert...

We don't cut corners

It takes talent and we've got it

The _____ experts

The _____'s best friend

You'll swear by us—not *at* us!

At _____, you're #1

Get hooked on _____

Go with a winner

It's easy to spot the winners

It's easy to see...

It's elementary...

Meet the newest addition to our family

The price cutters

There's no substitute for _____

The dependables

Train for the future

America's leading _____

America's favorite _____

The _____ pledge

A major breakthrough in _____

State-of-the-art _____

_____ is our middle name

Built to last

The fun begins with _____

Instant _____

_____ in your pocket

The smart choice

Don't get stuck with…

The _____ guys

Announcing the first…

Celebrate with _____

_____ where you want it, when you want it

Go all the way!

_____—for those who insist on the best

Finally, there's a better way to…

Nothing sells like a _____

Nothing's built like a _____

In a class by itself

_____ is our business

Don't gamble with…

Don't take chances with…

Take a chance with…

A _____ from the word "go"

The answer to your prayers

Who says you can't win 'em all?

The only way to…

Say "Yes!" to _____

Check us out

For those special times

For those special people in your life

How our _____ stacks up

Food for thought

Now, more than ever, you need _____

_____ reasons why you should…

So easy a child can do it

Everything you always wanted to know about _____

Can you afford *not* to…?

Don't wait for success to come to you!

Take a minute to…

An investment in your future

Your shortcut to…

Amazing medical breakthrough!

Turn your life around!

Other heads and slogans can be found under individual topics.

# Salutations and Invitations

Dear Friend:

Dear Neighbor:

Dear Customer:

Dear Preferred Customer:

Dear Valued Customer:

Dear Buyer:

Dear Patron of the Arts:

Dear Reader:

Dear Shareholder:

Dear Classmate:

Dear Fellow Alumnus:

Dear Subscriber:

Dear Retailer:

Dear Member:

Dear Citizen:

Greetings!

Attention!

Welcome to…

Come with us…

You are cordially invited…

A special invitation…

A personal invitation…

You are about to join…

Get ready to enjoy…

We request your presence…

You have been selected…

Join us…

We want you to…

Try this on for size:

# Opening with a Question

Isn't it time you…?

Did you know that…?

Are you still…?

Want to keep in touch with…?

Want to stay abreast of…?

Are you interested in…?

Are you curious about…?

Are you intrigued by…?

Will you be ready for the…?

Who could say no to…?

Do you want a better job?

Could you use an extra $_____ each month?

What's the best investment you could make?

How secure is your job?

Why postpone your future in…?

What would you say if we offered to help you…?

Will you risk just $1.00 to…?

Have you ever stayed awake at night thinking about…?

Did you ever ask yourself…?

How many times have you said to yourself, …?

Don't you need…?

Don't you wish…?

Wouldn't you like to…?

Why pay full price for _____ when you can buy for less at _____?

Confused about which _____ to buy?

Why should you use _____ when you can…?

Tired of empty promises from…?

Tired of the same old _____?

Why trade a _____ for a _____?

Why sacrifice _____ for _____?

Who can put a price on _____?

Are you ready for…?

Do you want to stretch your purchasing power?

How can you cut the high cost of _____?

How much is your company spending on _____?

Are you drowning in a sea of _____?

Have you ever thought about…?

What's the most effective way to…?

What's the most profitable…?

What's the safest…?

# Opening with a Statement

It's no secret that...

We'll change your mind about...

You've probably noticed that...

Just wait until you...

The results are in.

It's not every day that...

Forget everything you've heard about...

Imagine being able to get a _____ for only $ _____!

Just a note to tell you about...

Don't let _____ keep you from getting ahead.

_____ often spells the difference between failure and success.

Within 30 days from today, you could be...

You can organize a successful _____.

Think about...

Now you can...

For under $_____ you can...

You're the kind of person who...

Believe it or not, ...

You're in for a pleasant surprise.

If you're like most people, you probably...

If _____ is your passion, then you'll appreciate...

In today's competitive marketplace, ...

In today's uncertain economy, ...

We live in an increasingly complex society.

Today, more than ever, ...

It's a fact of life that...

It's never too early to...

It's never too late to...

Now, the real truth about...

Your new career in _____ is just weeks away.

Let us sell you on...

Anyone who knows _____ will tell you that...

It isn't enough to be...

Every once in a while you come across a _____ that...

_____ may determine the future of your business.

If you've been waiting for the right _____, you don't have to wait any longer.

It's hard enough to _____ without having to worry about _____.

Let's be honest.

Let's face it.

We've got the solution to your...

In the 10 seconds it took you to read this far, ...

If you'd like to become part of today's _____, there's no better way to start than...

# Opening with a Challenge

Take a giant step...

Do something extraordinary!

Be a winner!

Discover the...

Explore the...

Encounter the...

Experience the...

Meet the...

Learn about the...

Sample the...

Relive the...

Say "yes" to...

Join the...

Capture the...

Cross the threshold...

If you're seriously interested in...

If you sincerely want to...

Join the small handful of people who...

...like a professional!

Match wits with...

Match yourself against...

Make time for...

Return to the...

Delve into the...

Visit the...

Enjoy the...

Let your imagination soar!

Be your own (mechanic, plumber, etc.)!

If you think you're good enough...

# Snappy Transitions

Best of all, …

Fortunately, …

Here's why:

All this and more!

I'm hoping you fall into that category.

If questions like these intrigue you, …

And that's not all!

And there's more:

If you prefer, …

What does this mean for you?

Simply stated, …

In short, …

In brief, …

Let's look at the record:

As if that's not enough, …

What an opportunity!

We're sure you'll agree that…

Most important, …

Last but not least, …

So remember, …

So don't forget…

Now there's an even better way…

That's where _____ fits in.

One thing's for sure:

This we promise:

There you have it:

Think of it:

No doubt about it, …

That's why…

These are just a few of the…

You'll also be glad to know that…

As a further convenience, …

To show you what we mean, …

For the answer, turn this page.

We've saved the best news for last.

And this is only the beginning!

Now, for the first time, …

As if this weren't enough, …

And we don't stop there.

But there's even more.

But that's just part of the story.

The result?

No wonder…

Sounds incredible?

Sounds fantastic?

Fair enough?

…and that's the truth!

The truth is, …

The way we look at it, …

Now for the surprise:

What's more, …

# Other Grabbers

At last!

Fact:

Win...

Important!

Urgent!

Attention!

As seen on TV

Our loss is your gain!

Now you too can...

Now for the first time...

You may already have won!

By popular demand

This is your last chance to...

Hurry in for these...

Good news!

It's true!

Valuable document enclosed!

Exclusive!

Major breakthrough!

Grand opening!

Sneak preview!

New low price!

New!

Something to cheer about!

Treat yourself to a...

No problem!

You bet!

_____ reasons why you should buy...

Check these super features!

Here's what you get:

The first...

The only...

The first and only...

For further inspiration, see:
**Discount/Sale (Part 4)**
**Free/Prize (Part 4)**

# PART 2

# DESCRIPTIONS AND BENEFITS

Conveying the Value of Your Product or Service

# Appealing

irresistible

satisfying

charming

delightful

wonderful

enchanting

engaging

captivating

bewitching

piquant

moving

memorable

You'll fall in love with...

Experience the wonder of...

...beckons

You'll never forget...

gracious

unforgettable

just the right touch of...

the allure of...

never to be forgotten

a gem

an unexpected pleasure

felicitous

special

lovely

beguiling

pleasing

pleasant

winsome

lovable

huggable

cuddly

adorable

exquisite

enthralling

congenial

perfect

picture-perfect

picturesque

colorful

entertaining

alluring

fetching

inviting

---

For further inspiration, see:
**Comfortable**
**Exciting/Stimulating**
**Fabulous**
**Romantic**
**Sensory Qualities**

# Authentic

genuine

the real thing

honest-to-goodness

real-life

true-to-life

valid

legitimate

certified

backed by...

proven

tested

our reputation for...

realistic

lifelike

pure

true

faithful to

fidelity

the genuine article

the way _____ used to make it

the original _____

original formula

original recipe

old family recipe

accept no substitute

actual

the one and only

has stood the test of time

For further inspiration, see:
**Honest**
**Reliable/Solid**

# Big/Many

| | |
|---|---|
| enormous | a wealth of… |
| gigantic | lion's share |
| tremendous | stupendous |
| spectacular | rich |
| monumental | more _____ than any other… |
| massive | whopping |
| mammoth | generous |
| jumbo | oversized |
| immense | packed with… |
| sizable | lavish |
| king-size | boundless |
| titanic | towering |
| colossal | grand |
| huge | great |
| gargantuan | prodigious |
| Brobdingnagian | hefty |
| super _____ | substantial |
| a feast of… | voluminous |
| a gold mine of… | vast |
| a treasure trove of… | of epic proportion |
| a cornucopia of… | the biggest |
| a host of… | unlimited |
| a bonanza | the sky's the limit |
| abundant | an endless supply of… |
| an abundance of… | a full line of… |

a whale of a…

chock full of…

loaded with…

a myriad of…

This is just a partial list of…

an endless source of…

a rich source of…

abounds with…

a rich harvest of…

fruitful

luxuriant

\_\_\_\_\_ galore!

oodles of…

a multitude of…

numerous

countless

limitless

plentiful

ample

commodious

spacious

a profusion of…

profusely…

multiple…

filled with…

packed with…

a tremendous selection

Fur further inspiration, see:

**Complete**

**Powerful/Gripping**

# Color

| | |
|---|---|
| rose | chartreuse |
| burgundy | spring green |
| ruby | grass green |
| crimson | leaf green |
| scarlet | forest green |
| vermillion | parrot green |
| russet | lime |
| auburn | olive |
| copper | emerald |
| burnt orange | jade |
| sunset orange | turquoise |
| tangerine | aquamarine |
| pumpkin | cerulean |
| peach | cyan |
| apricot | ice blue |
| amber | sky blue |
| buff | azure |
| sandy | peacock blue |
| straw | sapphire |
| tawny | ultramarine |
| flaxen | navy |
| blond | midnight blue |
| lemon yellow | indigo |
| canary yellow | violet |
| goldenrod | grape |

| | |
|---|---|
| amethyst | steel gray |
| purple | ebony |
| plum | raven black |
| orchid | coal black |
| lilac | jet black |
| lavender | midnight black |
| mauve | blue-black |
| magenta | basic black |
| cerise | whiter-than-white |
| pink | brilliant white |
| shocking pink | winter white |
| coral | off-white |
| flesh | ivory |
| salmon | almond |
| sepia | cream |
| rust | alabaster |
| sienna | pearl |
| tan | silver |
| oak | pewter |
| mahogany | bronze |
| umber | gold |
| beige | antique gold |
| ecru | |
| taupe | |
| smoky gray | |

For further inspiration, see:
**Sensory Qualities**

# Comfortable

soothing

snug

comfy

cool and comfy

roomy

cheerful

peaceful

down-home

homey

relaxed

relaxing

restful

unhurried

casual

at ease

a haven of...

tranquil

serene

placid

hospitable

congenial

friendly

unassuming

all the comforts of home

Snuggle up with...

Cuddle up with...

Get comfortable with...

cuddly

cushiony

cottony soft

smooth as silk

velvety

You won't know you're wearing it.

loose-fitting

superb fit

firm support

just the way you like it

like walking on air

It breathes.

the latest in comfort

like floating on a cloud

soft as down

soft as a baby's bottom

cool as a summer breeze

air conditioned

warm as toast

For further inspiration, see:
**Appealing**
**Security/Peace of Mind**

# Complete/Thorough

comprehensive

A to Z

It's all here!

everything from _____ to _____

everything you need

the ultimate _____

the only _____ you'll ever need

in-depth

extensive

all-embracing

all-inclusive

all _____ included

exhaustive

scrupulously researched

a total...

the total...

the sum total...

everything you wanted to know about _____

everything under the sun

leaves no stone unturned

a complete package

complete in one package

panoramic

sweeping

encyclopedic

full-length

unabridged

uncut

unexpurgated

in its entirety

the all-in-one _____

built-in _____

completely integrated

complete with...

everything you've always wanted in a _____

all the features you'd expect

all the right ingredients

provides 100% of the _____ you need

furnishes all the _____ you need

---

For further inspiration, see:
**Big/Many**
**Superior**

# Convenient

right at your fingertips

within easy reach

handy

quick-reference

instant reference

all in one place

in your own home

no more endless searching

Never again will you have to...

combines the most outstanding features

Two _____ in one!

take it anywhere

versatile

facilitates

simplifies

clarifies

pushbutton convenience

armchair shopping

one-stop shopping

fast, easy access

strategically located

just a short stroll from...

located right in the heart of...

You won't have to shop around.

ready to go anywhere you are

easily adaptable

reproducible

pliable

maneuverable

accessible

fits your schedule

flexible design

direct from the manufacturer

transports easily

ships flat

fast setup

puts _____ in the palm of your hand

eliminates the need for...

even if you don't have...

Now you can order direct.

...at your convenience

for added mobility

easily adjustable

compatible with any _____

We're flexible when it comes to _____.

You could never duplicate it on your own.

just at the right time

whenever you want it

whenever you feel like...

It's there when you need it.

Choose only the ones you want.

takes the work out of...

makes _____ extra easy

opens the way to...

streamlines the...

For further inspiration, see:
**Easy**
**Service/Help**
**Useful/Suitable**

# Distinguished

significant

prize-winning

respected

a landmark

prestigious

major

premier

influential

a Who's Who of...

accomplished

vital

celebrated

eminent

illustrious

noted

notable

noteworthy

famous

renowned

the nation's leading...

the nation's most distinguished...

the nation's most respected...

the nation's most influential...

acclaimed

the ——— of record

prominent

world-class

the most talked about

the most imitated

a positive force in bringing about...

the leader in...

outstanding

honored

esteemed

revered

dominant

commanding

the absolute...

used by Fortune 500 companies

used by the people who count

a ——— of distinction

of high repute

high ranking

has won accolades

has won the respect of...

has played a major role in...

For further inspiration, see:
**Luxurious**
**Superior**
**Traditional/Classic**

# Easy

straightforward

step-by-step

amazingly simple

instant _____

at a glance

easy-to-follow

no prior _____ experience necessary

clearly and simply explained

great for beginners

You don't have to be an expert.

It's that simple!

in no time at all

no fussing

It's a snap...

It's a cinch...

It's a piece of cake.

It's a breeze.

It couldn't be easier.

no headaches

uncomplicated

safe and simple

so easy a child can do it

child's play

All you do is...

It's never been easier to...

You'll discover how easy it is to...

_____ the easy way

easier than ever before

simplified

intelligible

clear

clearly written

written in plain English

fast-reading

easy to understand

jargon-free

user-friendly

...coasting all the way

no sweat

foolproof

effortless

manageable

within minutes

fast

quick

one-step _____

all in one easy step

easy as one, two, three

accessible

so advanced, it's actually simple

one touch and it…

easy-to-assemble

installs in seconds

ready-to-use

ready-to-go

smooth sailing

practically runs itself

For further inspiration, see:
**Convenient**

# Exciting/Stimulating

provocative

entertaining

amusing

lively

vibrant

colorful

vivid

sizzling

shocking

tingling

stunning

striking

arresting

startling

thought-provoking

candid

fascinating

intriguing

incisive

rousing

stirring

seductive

alluring

titillating

tempting

tantalizing

spicy

piquant

racy

heady

Wow!

a knockout

explosive

overwhelming

dramatic

thrilling

engrossing

sensational

astonishing

spellbinding

mesmerizing

breathtaking

hair-raising

spine-tingling

intoxicating

galvanizing

electrifying

staggering

revealing

an adventure in...

enlivened by...

bold

imaginative

no-holds-barred

exhilarating

challenging

compelling

absorbing

a humdinger

dynamic

gripping

never lets up

For further inspiration, see:
**Appealing**
**Fabulous**
**Fresh/Wholesome**
**Fun**
**New/Advanced**
**Pleasure/Satisfaction**
**Sensory Qualities**

# Experienced/Expert

talented

qualified

accomplished

authoritative

professional

veteran

ace

a team of experts

our award-winning staff

our professional staff

a crack team of...

We're professionals.

We're pros.

...have combined their talents

...have pooled their expertise

professional expertise

We're the original _____.

for over _____ years

since (date)

pioneers in...

solid experience

seasoned

talent for...

flair for...

mastery of...

masters at...

masterly

the artistry of...

the wizardry of...

craftsmanship

skilled

trained

capable

gifted

endowed with...

well-versed in...

virtuoso

genius for...

ingenious

ingenuity

talent and imagination

the stamp of creativity

We've got the right stuff.

We've got the talent.

We have vision.

We invented...

We developed...

We pioneered the...

We're the ones who...

We had the foresight to...

We've shaped the growth of…

We have first-hand experience with…

We're thoroughly familiar with…

competence

imagination

finesse

proficiency

professionalism

top-flight

top-drawer

_____ is our strong suit.

_____ is our specialty.

For further inspiration, see:
**Reliable/Solid**
**Results**
**Superior**

**Enhancing Your Company's Image**
**(Part 5)**
**Knocking the Competition (Part 5)**

# Fabulous

magnificent

dazzling

splendid

breathtaking

sublime

spectacular

sensational

sumptuous

opulent

majestic

elegant

fantastic

awesome

awe-inspiring

striking

monumental

wonderful

marvelous

remarkable

superb

glorious

exalted

a towering achievement

great

terrific

stunning

sparkling

glittering

a bravura performance

the kind of _____ you've only dreamed about

undreamed of

incredible

amazing

...will amaze you.

unforgettable

---

For further inspiration, see:
**Exciting/Stimulating**
**Fun**
**Luxurious**
**Sensory Qualities**
**Superior**

# Fresh/Wholesome

springtime fresh

light (lite)

light as air

soft

dainty

pastel-colored

flowery

clean

mild

sealed-in freshness

fresh scent

fragrant

a bouquet of...

a breath of...

a summer breeze

natural

all-natural

organically grown

homemade

homespun

old-fashioned goodness

oven-fresh

sunshine fresh

whiter-than-white

immaculate

cool and crisp

brisk

zesty

refreshing

bracing

rejuvenating

invigorating

exhilarating

a tonic

will revive your...

will renew your...

will make you feel brand new

the way nature made it

nothing artificial

no additives

untainted by...

pristine

from the earth

pine scented

lemon scented

the fragrance of wildflowers

For further inspiration, see:
**Appealing**
**Comfortable**
**Exciting/Stimulating**
**Sensory Qualities**

# Fun

amusing

hilarious

entertaining

rollicking

festive

diverting

merry

jolly

giddy

gay

sunny

playful

convivial

carefree

relaxing

a romp

a caper

escapades

pleasure

hedonism

merriment

hilarity

mirth

gaiety

revelry

orgy

just for kicks

just for laughs

laugh-a-minute

frolic

carouse

make merry

Go on a spree!

Paint the town!

Live it up!

Indulge yourself.

Enjoy!

laugh it up

giggle

chuckle

chortle

guffaw

belly laughs

tickles your funny bone

knee-slapping

a riot

a laugh riot

The fun begins with _____.

Let yourself go.

Get away from it all.

enjoyed by all

for pleasure seekers

hedonism *plus*

good times

a barrel of laughs

rolling in the aisles

cavorting

a circus

a bacchanal

a pleasure feast

a celebration

an extravaganza

festivities

recreation

revels

For further inspiration, see:
**Exciting/Stimulating**
**Pleasure/Satisfaction**

# Honest

straight talk about...

the plain truth

nothing but the truth

truthful

the truth about _____

candid

frank

straightforward

uninhibited

outspoken

forthright

up-front

tells it like it is

integrity

no-holds-barred

hard-hitting

revealing

point-blank

unequivocal

sincere

open

direct

genuine

plain English

jargon-free

cold hard facts

just the facts

reputable

reliable

factual information

We offer proof.

We explode the myths about _____.

We probe...

We uncover...

We unmask...

We don't pull punches.

We strip away the...

an exposé of...

the nitty-gritty

a critical eye

honest-to-goodness

Let's be honest about...

For further inspiration, see:
**Authentic**
**Reliable/Solid**

**Enhancing Your Company's Image
(Part 5)**

# Improved

newly redesigned

newly revised

better than ever

the first real improvement in _____
since...

You'll find more to like than ever before.

Times are changing and so are we.

a time to grow and change

new, improved _____

now with more _____

increased _____

changed

expanded

enriched

enhanced

a new look

new design

new refinements

modified

refurbished

remodeled

restored

reformed

renewed

revived

reorganized

restructured

re-created

refined

beautified

spruced up

perfected

the best just got better

We've made great strides...

We've bettered...

We've transformed ...

We've changed the rules...

a change for the better

new blood

a renaissance

a metamorphosis in the making

an about-face

We're growing to serve you better.

Of course, we'll continue to...

For further inspiration, see:
**New/Advanced**

# Indispensable

a "must"

a necessity

invaluable

the bible of...

the _____ no family should be without

an indispensable tool

essential

an essential ingredient

imperative

obligatory

important

significant

crucial

critical

urgent

consequential

a prerequisite

basic

the primary...

the chief...

the principal...

the foundation of...

the heart of...

the key to...

the nerve center of...

Don't _____ without it!

You'll wonder how you ever got along without it.

Don't you think you need _____?

the basis of any good _____

vital

a vital link

---

For further inspiration, see:
**Reliable/Solid**
**Superior**
**Useful/Suitable**

# Informative

instructive

educational

illuminating

enlightening

eye-opening

mind-opening

keeps you abreast of...

keeps you in touch with...

keeps you informed

...while it informs

expands your knowledge

alters your perceptions

stirs the imagination

will familiarize you with...

gives you an insider's grasp of...

will stretch your mind

superb ideas for...

takes the guesswork out of...

takes the mystery out of...

unlocks the secrets of...

the answers you've always wanted

the answers to these and hundreds of other questions

everything you always wanted to know about...

...that you ought to know about

keeps you ahead of the game

gives you the hard facts

helps you separate fact from fiction

gives you the facts you need to make important decisions

a unique learning experience

will open up new channels of information

satisfies your need to know

gives you new insight

instant feedback

For further inspiration, see:
**Complete**
**Exciting/Stimulating**
**Honest**
**Self-Improvement**
**Service/Help**

# Luxurious

| | |
|---|---|
| plush | museum quality |
| ornate | masterpiece |
| opulent | craftsmanship |
| deluxe | finely crafted |
| only the finest… | hand-tooled |
| sumptuous | intricate |
| ambrosial | delicate tracery |
| epicurean | limited edition |
| precious | rare |
| embellished | fancy |
| glittering | exquisite |
| the glint of gold | valuable |
| gemlike | invaluable |
| gilt-edged | treasured |
| gilded | superior |
| splendid | elite |
| superb | posh |
| magnificent | elegantly appointed |
| first class | individually crafted |
| VIP | specially commissioned |
| upscale | _____ signifies quality |
| refined | worthy of royalty |
| fine grained | go in style |
| elegant | charm and grandeur |
| classic | a _____ of obvious distinction |

beautiful accoutrements

becomes more precious with time

quality that suits your style of living

always in perfect taste

spoils you for anything else

caters to the discriminating few

all the amenities

excellence

for those who demand excellence

where excellence is a tradition

For further inspiration, see:
**Fabulous**
**Status**
**Stylish**
**Superior**
**Justifying a High Price (Part 5)**

# Money-Making

_____ your way to riches!

money-making opportunity

Make money the easy way!

Double your earnings!

Make a million in _____.

Do you sincerely want to make a million?

Dozens of money-making opportunities!

Turn your _____ into gold!

a golden opportunity

Profit from...

Cash in on...

Make a bundle...

Get rich without going to work!

...will pay big dividends.

the fast track to wealth

undreamed-of riches

pays off

the payoff

high yields

Triple your investment in _____ years!

tax-free earnings

multiplies your investment

Watch your money grow.

Protect your investment.

Create interest.

Build your nest egg.

for the aggressive investor

growth potential

a smart investment

a wise investment

the opportunity of a lifetime

unlimited earnings

top dollar

top salary

megabucks

money in the bank

good as gold

a 3-step formula that guarantees success

my personal formula for wealth

guaranteed formula

Make a fortune in direct mail!

Run a successful _____ business in your spare time.

Earn $_____ a month in your spare time!

Earn $_____ your first year!

Rack up profits.

easy profits

overnight profits

profit leaders

profitable

new profit sources

Reach profitable new markets.

high turnover

cold cash

hot sellers

bestsellers

perennial bestsellers

They sell themselves!

sizzling sales

Your commissions will multiply…

Watch your profits soar!

guaranteed to boost sales

Over _____ million sold!

a hot item

keeps on selling

generates profits

For further inspiration, see:
**Money-Saving**
**Self-Improvement**

# Money-Saving

a fabulous bargain

tremendous savings

extra value

pays for itself

marked down

inexpensive

thrifty

low cost

big value

extra savings

your money's worth

You get more for your dollar.

economical

packed full of value

the best deal in town

fits your budget

easy on your pocketbook

incredible values

a terrific value

Compare our prices with...

Imagine being able to get a _____ for only $_____!

And you thought you couldn't afford _____!

Finally, a _____ you can afford.

First-class _____ at no-frills prices!

designer quality at affordable prices

You save because...

No middleman!

You'll save a few dollars in the bargain.

Our loss is your gain!

money-saving ideas

money-saving opportunity

the best _____ for your money

a truckload of savings

remarkable cash savings

affordable

surprisingly affordable

invitingly priced

at popular prices

rock-bottom prices

a fraction of the original price

unheard-of low prices

Pick up a bargain.

You'll never find another bargain like this one!

Get ready for fantastic savings.

like getting three _____s for the price of one

Only $_____ entitles you to...

a modest investment

You won't believe this price!

Anywhere else you could expect to pay up to $_____!

a best buy

a best bet

Save on _____ costs.

cost-efficient

no wasted expense

a full-time staff at part-time cost

cuts costs dramatically

helps you avoid costly mistakes

eliminates costly _____

cuts your overhead costs

...on a shoestring budget

For further inspiration, see:
**Other Grabbers (Part 1)**
**Discount/Sale (Part 4)**

# New/Advanced

contemporary

innovative

the latest

state-of-the-art

groundbreaking

trailblazing

brand new

bold new

remarkable new

revolutionary

modern

ultramodern

up-to-date

up-to-the-minute

high-tech

sophisticated

scientifically developed

current

latest technology

futuristic

21st century

today's _____

designed for today's _____

keeps pace with...

something new and exciting

makes the _____ obsolete

an exciting new way to...

space age _____

the first and only

a revolution in _____

a breakthrough in _____

the successor to _____

right out of tomorrow

a whole new world of _____

a radical departure

a novel approach

unprecedented

adds a new dimension to _____

the world's first _____

for tomorrow's business needs

now and new

computer technology

technologically advanced

second generation _____

topical

the _____ of the future

You'll know you've seen the future.

where everything is happening

new horizons

the new look in _____

Introducing…

Coming soon…

a totally new concept in _____

a new era

in the vanguard

precision _____

modular

just released

just published

now available

available for the first time

another first

a great new idea

a fresh approach to _____

For further inspiration, see:
**Improved**
**Timely**

# Pleasure/Satisfaction

Imagine the fun you'll have...

the time of your life

your passport to...

entertains while it...

enjoyment for years to come

...will revive your senses

Try a little self-indulgence.

to delight the eye

satisfies your need for...

great family fun

a wealth of activities

sparks enthusiasm

Get more out of...

satisfies your hunger

hits the spot

Taste the difference!

will make you feel good all over

will make you brand new again

will provide countless hours of
entertainment

will delight every member of the family

will captivate you

You'll be tickled...

You'll love...

You'll enjoy...

You'll appreciate...

You'll delight in...

...to your heart's content

your utmost enjoyment

made for you to enjoy

Sit back and enjoy...

deeply satisfying

gratifying

delightful to give or receive

years of enjoyment

Get in on the fun.

For once in your life, live!

For further inspiration, see:
**Appealing**
**Exciting/Stimulating**
**Fun**
**Luxurious**
**Sensory Qualities**

**Guarantees (Part 4)**

# Popular

acclaimed

best-selling

favorite

all-time favorite

America's favorite

famous

famed

legendary

celebrated

illustrious

in vogue

the ____ sensation

the ____ phenomenon

the ____ bandwagon

the ____ Age

word-of-mouth popularity

preferred by more...

attended by more...

bought by more...

recommended by more...

approved by...

endorsed by...

chosen by...

always in demand

widespread acceptance

has struck a responsive chord

one of the most talked-about ____

Everybody's talking about ____.

More and more ____ are discovering ____.

Everybody loves ____.

a winner

a superstar

a blockbuster

triumphant

the hottest ____ in town

the people's choice

renowned

world-renowned

world-famous

known far and wide

flourishing

thriving

booming

a fabulous success

phenomenally successful

a success story

You can't argue with success.

---

For further inspiration, see:
**Distinguished**
**Stylish**

# Powerful/Gripping

explosive

dynamite

a knockout

gut-wrenching

overwhelming

high-powered

intense

potent

mighty

dynamic

forceful

elemental

mindblowing

high-voltage

electric

electrifying

unyielding

unrelenting

overpowering

Herculean

titanic

Promethean

muscular

sinewy

masterful

commanding

compelling

staggering

riveting

mesmerizing

shocking

stunning

vibrant

packs a wallop

packs a punch

never lets up

knocks your socks off

vitality

vigor

energy

primitive power

raw power

For further inspiration, see:
**Exciting/Stimulating**

# Reliable/Solid

no-nonsense

practical

functional

strong

high-performance

heavyweight

rugged

tough

durable

dependable

stands up to...

comes to grips with...

our proven method of...

proven techniques

gets the job done when you need it

a lifetime of satisfaction

will last for generations

lasts a lifetime

carefully tested

laboratory tested

reinforced

precision engineered

ruggedly built

made to last

built to last

heavy-duty

high-impact

virtually indestructible

will never let you down

made to exacting specifications

quality controlled

stringent standards

rigorous standards

our high standards

individually tested

_____ can handle it

We don't cut corners.

no compromising on quality

no shortcuts

smooth performance

tamper-proof

a proven track record

_____ never lets you down.

the quality you've come to expect

top credentials

sound

valid

trusted

unswerving

faithful to...

secure

firm

stable

surefire

error-free

established

time-tested

For further inspiration, see:
**Authentic**
**Experienced/Expert**
**Honest**
**Results**
**Security/Peace of Mind**

**Enhancing Your Company's Image
(Part 5)**

# Results

unmatched performance

instant _____

fast-acting

works immediately

works wonders

works like magic

It really works!

gets the job done

does the job

does the trick

fast results

remarkable results

instant results

proven results

gets results

makes the difference

success guaranteed

You can count on _____.

never lets you down

comes through in the clutch

increases

boosts

acts

performs

accomplishes

never lets up

produces

delivers

delivers the goods

improves

raises

lowers

maintains

provides

furnishes

restores

revitalizes

protects

stops

cuts down on

reduces

prevents

creates

corrects

fixes

cuts through

does it all

high-efficiency

effective

pays off

Compare for yourself.

Find out for yourself.

Watch it go to work!

outperforms the competition

does more with less

changes unproductive habits

boosts morale

builds motivation

increases productivity

helps build a top-performing team

For further inspiration, see:
**Experienced/Expert**
**Reliable/Solid**
**Service/Help**

# Romantic

enchanting

haunting

enthralling

evocative

captivating

mystical

magical

dreamlike

a storybook world

Set the mood for...

Enter a timeless realm of...

Surrender to the spell of...

creates an aura of...

the eternal mystery of...

a wondrous journey

enchanted places

life's most treasured moments

the romance of...

passionate

breathless

intimate

kindled

burning

smoldering

torrid

rapturous

ravishing

For further inspiration, see:
**Appealing**
**Sensory Qualities**
**Traditional/Classic**

# Security/Peace of Mind

full protection

total security

total privacy

secluded

safe

a haven of...

a bulwark against...

shelters you from...

insulates you...

guards you against...

your assurance of...

your guarantee of...

your defense against...

puts your mind at ease

saves you needless worry

protects you

You won't lose any more sleep over...

You'll never again have to worry about...

Relax!

Take it easy!

takes care of itself

Sleep secure.

You can rest easy.

You can depend on...

You can count on...

You can rely on...

protects your valuable _____

protects your investment

no more guesswork

a lifetime of _____

lets you forget about...

You're in control.

_____ with confidence.

We're always there when you need us.

Your _____ can never be canceled.

For further inspiration, see:
**Comfortable**
**Reliable/Solid**

**Guarantees (Part 4)**

# Self-Improvement

self-expression

self-esteem

self-confidence

self-worth

self-mastery

growth

wisdom

harmony

fulfillment

knowledge

education

Move ahead...

Move on...

You owe yourself...

You can do it!

Go for it!

succeed

strive

pursue

win

Live your dreams.

You've dreamed about it. Now you can *do* it!

Opportunity knocks!

a golden opportunity

a new you

awakens your spirit

unleashes your creativity

an investment in your future

your chance to...

opens the way to...

will give you a whole new perspective

You'll feel confident...

Live more confidently!

expands your horizons

skills you will use your whole life long

a chance to use your talents

You'll be glad you did.

Gain hands-on experience...

_____ can be the key to your success.

We'll stretch your mind.

You'll learn by doing.

practical, hands-on training

gives you a clear advantage

gives you the competitive edge

keeps you ahead of the game

gets you in on the ground floor

You start with _____ and quickly move on to _____.

You'll feel good about yourself.

You'll feel as good as you look.

You'll look like a million.

infinite possibilities

Reach your full potential.

Discover your hidden talents.

Unlock your potential.

Remove mental blocks to success.

the road to success

Success can be yours!

Be the success you were meant to be.

Wake up the _____ inside you.

In _____ weeks you can be on your way to...

Turn your life around.

Invest in yourself.

---

For further inspiration, see:
**Exciting/Stimulating**
**Informative**

**Heads and Slogans (Part 1)**

# Sensory Qualities

gorgeous

sensuous

elegant

handsome

shapely

attractive

appealing

alluring

dazzling

vivid

splendid

tempting

titillating

tantalizing

intimate

sheer

sleek

sexy

ripe

voluptuous

tropical

warm

radiant

sunswept

windswept

rainbow-colored

crystalline

icy

cool

creamy

textured

burnished

luminous

incandescent

glowing

moonlit

sunlit

earthy

soothing

whisper-soft

graceful

contoured

moist

firm

rounded

oval

liquid

effervescent

sparkling

glittering

| | |
|---|---|
| fiery | zesty |
| fire and ice | seasoned with... |
| hot | luscious |
| white-hot | delicious |
| brilliant | delectable |
| clean | sweet |
| harmonious | salty |
| fragrant | spicy |
| bouquet | subtle |
| aromatic | melodious |
| musky | resonant |
| savory | echoing |
| mouthwatering | ringing |
| tasty | pealing |
| crisp | jingling |
| crunchy | chiming |
| chewy | trilling |
| flaky | warbling |
| tender | whistling |
| juicy | billowing |
| succulent | thundering |
| ambrosial | calm |
| tangy | tranquil |
| tart | paradise |
| pungent | a garden of delights |

the scent of roses

a field of daffodils

alpine meadows

a rushing brook

a waterfall

a crystal pool

the wind in the trees

a thunderstorm

the sound of rain on the roof

the pounding surf

salt spray

sun and sand

a tropical sunrise/sunset

purple shadows

a summer night

For further inspiration, see:
**Appealing**
**Color**
**Fresh/Wholesome**
**Pleasure/Satisfaction**

# Service/Help

helps you...

lets you...

permits you to...

assists you...

aids

solves

monitors

advises

creates

performs

We deliver...

Our job is to help you...

That's what we give you.

We do the work for you.

sound advice on how to...

professional advice

personal advice

guides you every step of the way

Let _____ show you the right way to...

Let us pamper you.

a good friend to have by your side

We make an effort to...

We do it all for you.

We come to your aid.

the solution to your...

We cater to...

prompt service

instant feedback

Your _____ gets top-priority treatment.

We provide training and support.

Our friendly staff is ready to assist you.

...to serve you better

Each of our dealers is hand-picked...

Your _____ dealer goes out of his way to...

Your _____ dealer will work with you...

Your _____ dealer takes the time and effort to...

Your _____ dealer makes himself available...

Let _____ plan and manage your _____.

We work harder to make it happen for you.

At _____, we do all that and more.

We make it easier for you to...

We're in business to help your business succeed.

You can turn to us with confidence.

...when, where, and for as long as you need it

the answer to all your _____ needs

We offer a full range of...

We'll meet all your requirements.

evaluation

review

consultation

assessment

design

technical assistance

technical support

proposals

conversion

testing

tracking

locating

estimating

scheduling

costing

billing

training

implementation

documentation

debugging

installation

enhancements

modifications

projections

distribution

precision marketing

inventory management

site selection

breadth of service

one-stop assistance

first-hand briefing

a professional recommendation

a total management tool

For further inspiration, see:
**Convenient**
**Experienced/Expert**
**Indispensable**
**Reliable/Solid**
**Results**

# Small/Less

fits easily in your _____

takes up only _____ of space

space-saving

miniature

mini-

micro-

compact styling

neat

concise

brief

compact

cozy

intimate

delicate

pocket-sized

midget

dwarf

pygmy

elfin

Lilliputian

cute

_____ in your pocket

portable

Take it wherever you go.

fits anywhere

in a nutshell

condensed

abridged

vest-pocket

scaled-down

diminutive

tiny

minute

petite

a dash of...

a pinch of...

a little bit of...

a soupçon of...

greatly reduced

reduced to a minimum

barely more than...

virtually nonexistent

smaller and lighter

wispy

lightweight

light as a feather

diminished

compressed

slim

For further inspiration, see:
**Convenient**

# Status

prestige

cachet

class

rank

highest ranking

selective

competitive

discriminating

private

exclusive

elite

aristocratic

among the elect

in good standing

the creme de la creme

a prestigious address

the Rolls-Royce of _____

You'll join the ranks of...

You'll join a very select group.

You'll be in on...

automatically entitles you to...

connects you with...

gives you an insider's grasp of...

VIP treatment

identifies you as...

members-only

You'll be privy to...

belongs in the home of every educated person

will confer upon its owner...

recognized by cultured people everywhere

found only in museums and distinguished private collections

You'll be welcomed.

You'll beam with pride.

Until now, only a fortunate few have been able to...

a behind-the-scenes look

gives you a privileged glimpse...

the value of a _____ address

Don't settle for anything less than _____.

For further inspiration, see:
**Distinguished**
**Luxurious**
**Stylish**

**Flattering the Reader (Part 5)**
**Using Demographics to Impress (Part 5)**

# Stylish

glamorous

chic

smart

elegant

hot

the hottest _____ in town

smashing

snazzy

sassy

new look

fashionable

with panache

pizzazz

flair

that certain "je ne sais quoi"

well bred

high society

classy

worldly

in vogue

a la mode

the last word in _____

the latest

current

trendy

all the rage

sleek

slinky

slim

slender

svelte

dashing

dapper

debonair

suave

sophisticated

savoir faire

natty

rakish

funky

Outasight!

outrageous

daring

bold

Ivy League

preppy

well tailored

designer _____

splashy

flashy

dressed to kill

coordinated

the right stuff

correct

tasteful

classically simple

graceful

sporty

distinctive

For further inspiration, see:
**Luxurious**
**New/Advanced**
**Status**

# Superior

highest quality

the finest...

the greatest...

the foremost...

unsurpassed

surpassingly...

first class

first-rate

brilliant

excellent

elite

outstanding

superlative

superb

distinguished

America's number one _____

America's leading _____

the aristocrat of _____

the definitive _____

the ultimate _____

the choicest _____

the apex

the summit

top-of-the-line

the best in the business

the undisputed leader

unbeatable

nobody beats...

the leading...

the top...

tops

top-ranking

matchless

unmatched

unrivaled

unexcelled

unparalleled

peerless

incomparable

paramount

preeminent

still the best

top-notch

your number one source

impeccable

perfect

sets the standard

in a class by itself

outclasses

surpasses

excels

outranks

outshines

premium quality

the standard by which other _____ are
judged

the best in the industry

the best anywhere

the finest _____ you can own

nobody else comes close

the better way to...

more than all others combined

transcends the common _____

second to none

supreme

For further inspiration, see:
**Big/Many**
**Complete/Thorough**
**Distinguished**
**Improved**
**Luxurious**
**Reliable/Solid**

**Enhancing Your Company's Image**
**(Part 5)**
**Justifying a High Price (Part 5)**
**Knocking the Competition (Part 5)**

# Timely

a welcome addition to...

long-awaited

long overdue

long-needed

At last there's a...

just when you need it most

the _____ whose time has come

Do we need it now!

Now is the time for...

There's never been a better time for...

It was only a matter of time.

Just when you thought...

It's finally here.

just in time for _____

It's about time...

Isn't it time...?

There's no time like the present.

_____ came along at just the right time.

the first _____ to address the problems of...

For further inspiration, see:
**Improved**
**New/Advanced**

# Traditional/Classic

legendary

historic

age-old

centuries-old

antique

the storied past

in the rich tradition of…

evokes a world of…

redolent of another age

the beauty of a vanished world

treasured heirloom

keepsake

masterpieces

old masters

nostalgic

a nostalgic glimpse of…

quaint

hallmarks of…

in the beginning…

It's an old _____ custom.

the legacy of…

heritage

roots

history comes alive

richly restored

timeless

immortal

vintage

never goes out of style

enduring quality

---

For further inspiration, see:
**Distinguished**
**Experienced/Expert**
**Luxurious**
**Romantic**

# Unusual

unique

the only...

a different kind of _____

unprecedented

uncommon

unconventional

distinctive

exclusive

rare

remarkable

daring

exceptional

unlike any other...

custom designed

one of a kind

...with a difference

a fresh approach to...

refreshingly different

a refreshing change of pace

an exciting change of pace

_____ with a twist!

_____ with a different spirit

something new and different

out of the ordinary

There's nothing quite like it.

matchless

incomparable

original

uniquely suited to...

specially formulated

the first and only...

extraordinary

hard to find

off the beaten track

the one and only...

not available in any store

Nobody else gives you...

We searched far and wide for these...

Only _____ brings you...

Only _____ offers you...

one of those _____ you encounter only a few times during your life

in a class by itself

the only one of its kind

a rare find

No other _____ comes close.

___

For further inspiration, see:
**Exciting/Stimulating
New/Advanced**

# Useful/Suitable

functional

practical

applicable

adaptable

flexible

versatile

multipurpose

helpful

worthwhile

usable

handy

just right

ideal for...

perfect for...

the perfect complement to...

a perfect match

equally suitable for _____ as well as _____

uniquely suited...

It was made for you.

We're sure to have the perfect _____ for you.

the ideal companion to...

created especially for you

becomes you

fits you like a glove

designed specifically for...

the _____ you've been looking for

an expression of your...

designed for the _____ in you

It's the real you.

compatible with...

can be integrated with your existing _____

can serve as a _____ as well as a _____

can be used in...

fast and easy to use

utilizes your...

...for all your needs

for every purpose

suited to your purpose

serves a useful purpose

tailored to your needs

designed to suit your needs

geared to your needs

custom-designed

customized

personalized

perfect for school, home, or office

serves as a _____

doubles as a _____

for every purpose

a wide variety of uses

all-purpose

For further inspiration, see:
**Convenient**
**Indispensable**
**Service/Help**
**Timely**

# PART 3
# CLINCHERS

Closing Statements that Motivate the Reader to Respond

# Persuading the Reader

Why settle for _____ when you can have _____?

You'll want to add it to your personal collection.

_____ belongs in the home of every educated family.

You'll receive all these benefits:

You can't lose.

What have you got to lose?

In short, you've got nothing to lose.

This is the opportunity you've been waiting for.

A rewarding _____ awaits you.

Can you think of any reason *not* to send for your _____?

You owe it to your family to…

Frankly, I can't understand why *everybody* doesn't take advantage of this offer.

We think you'll find that…

We think you'll agree…

We stand behind our claims.

We're ready to prove everything we claim.

When every dollar counts, it's good to know that…

Your gift is tax-deductible.

I know you receive appeals from many good causes, but I can't think of a better cause than…

We need you…you need us!

Does all this sound too good to be true?

You'll still be able to do it your way—only better!

Before you buy a _____, find out what _____ has to offer.

You'll wonder how you ever managed without it.

We're sure to have the perfect _____ for you.

You won't be disappointed.

Put your _____ to the test.

Seeing is believing.

That's all it takes to…

All this can be yours.

Take as many as you wish—or none at all!

You can see for yourself that…

Once you try us, you'll want to stay with us.

Our supply is limited.

In the last analysis, all that matters is…

Remember, time is running out.

Take advantage of this special offer.

You'll be glad you did.

Try to imagine the alternative.

Think of what you have to look forward to!

You've waited long enough.

You'll wonder why you waited.

…and that's a promise!

There's just one conclusion:

_____ is the obvious choice.

It's no wonder that we're the number one
choice…

For further inspiration, see:
**Guarantees (Part 4)**
**Trial Offer/No Obligation (Part 4)**

# The Moment of Decision

This is your moment!

Now is the best time!

You can do it!

Don't wait any longer!

Don't hesitate!

Don't miss out!

Don't miss this opportunity!

Why wait another day?

Why forego the pleasure?

You've waited long enough.

We're expecting you.

We need you.

Now it's time for you to decide.

It's a winning decision.

Take this important first step.

Decide for yourself!

See for yourself.

Say "yes" to...

Act now!

Don't delay!

But don't just take our word for it. Find out for yourself!

Interested?

Intrigued?

Convinced?

You'll just have to experience it for yourself.

Make this the turning point of your life.

Order now while there's still time.

We're expecting you.

Put our ideas to work!

Check it out.

Rather than simply reading about it, why don't you...?

You be the judge.

It's time to make your choice.

You've got an important decision to make.

It's up to you.

There's no time like the present!

Time's running out!

Do it today!

But do it now!

Reserve your _____ today!

# Making Contact

We're looking forward to seeing you.

We look forward to hearing from you.

May I hear from you soon?

I can't wait to hear from you.

We'd like to hear from you.

Just drop us a letter.

Ask your _____ dealer.

Send for our colorful catalog.

Send for our free catalog.

Mail your order today!

Get all the facts.

Write for our free illustrated brochure.

Send in your application today!

Mail this convenient coupon today!

An order form is enclosed for your convenience.

Just fill out the convenient order form.

Please return it to me at your earliest convenience.

For more details call your...

Call us today. We're in the white (yellow) pages.

We're waiting for your call.

In a hurry? Call...

For even faster service, call...

Why not give us a call and find out more about us?

Please don't hesitate to call us.

Call our toll-free number.

_____ is just a phone call away.

Just reach for your phone.

Call us this week to schedule an appointment.

For a free demonstration call...

Hurry in for a demonstration.

Come in and introduce yourself!

Come visit us at your convenience.

Come in and let us show you around.

We'll be glad to show you around.

Let us visit you at your convenience.

Our representative will call you at your convenience.

Your _____ dealer has all the details.

For further inspiration, see:
**Following Through (Part 5)**

# PART 4
# TERMS AND OFFERS

Making the "Bottom Line" Irresistible

# Discount/Sale

Double your savings!

Half price!

New low price!

Save up to _____%!

_____% off!

_____% discount!

drastic reductions on...

spectacular savings

marked down to...

extra savings

Price break!

Prices slashed!

We've rolled back prices!

Lowest prices ever!

huge discounts

substantial savings

tremendous savings

We've cut prices on...

a steal at these prices

We must move our inventory.

Everything must go!

Final clearance!

One-day sale!

One day only!

Take an extra 20% off the ticketed price!

Prices guaranteed through _____.

Fall preview sale!

Now only $_____!

Compare prices!

Shop and compare!

Special purchase!

carnival of values

a carnival of savings

For a limited time only!

Giant closeout sale!

Go on a shopping spree!

biggest discounts anywhere

We will not be undersold!

We'll beat any price!

We dare you to find lower prices anywhere!

No lower prices anywhere!

Lowest prices allowed by law!

Don't pay more!

Comparable _____ currently sell for $_____ or more.

No lower rates available anywhere!

at a substantial savings you can't afford to pass up

These _____ represent a superb value.

Check the savings.

Every _____ on sale!

Take advantage of this offer while it lasts!

You may never see a bargain like this one again!

Special introductory offer!

Special get-acquainted offer!

Exclusive offer!

Rebate!

For further inspiration, see:
**Other Grabbers (Part 1)**
**Money-Saving (Part 2)**

# Free/Prize

yours FREE

absolutely FREE

Claim your free _____!

free of charge

at no charge

Valuable gift enclosed!

Free gift!

Free gift enclosed!

We're giving away...

It's yours to keep.

Keep it, use it, enjoy it!

Accept this...

To further enhance your pleasure, you
will receive a _____ at no extra charge.

Send for free facts.

This one's on us!

included at no extra cost

It's yours FREE just for saying "yes" to...

Take it—it's yours!

It's our way of saying "thank you."

early bird bonus

Win...

Play and win!

Double your winnings!

Over _____ chances to win!

Take your pick of these fabulous prizes!

All prizes will be awarded!

Win a brand-new _____!

hundreds of prizes

For further inspiration, see:
**Other Grabbers (Part 1)**
**Money-Saving (Part 2)**

# Trial Offer/No Obligation

Send no money now!

Send no payment now!

Send no money!

No risk!

No risk now, no risk later!

No-risk trial offer!

30-day free trial!

No obligation to buy anything ever!

No strings attached!

Use it for a week in your own home.

You may cancel at any time.

Say "yes" now and decide later.

If you decide to keep it, pay just $_____.

If I decide to keep it, I will pay just $_____.

Choose only the _____ you want.

Keep only the _____ you want.

You may cancel at any time, simply by notifying us.

If you decide not to..., pay nothing and keep the _____ with our compliments.

No purchase necessary!

No down payment!

No salesman will call.

Try us for six months.

All we're asking is that you give us a try.

a fair trial

Try us on for size.

What have you got to lose?

Try _____ at our risk.

We'll buy it back—no questions asked!

We'll send you _____ to examine FREE—no cost, obligation, or commitment.

For further inspiration, see:
**Guarantees**

**Persuading the Reader (Part 3)**

# Guarantees

satisfaction guaranteed

fully guaranteed

unconditional money-back guarantee

unconditionally guaranteed

ironclad guarantee

We back it up with a _____ guarantee.

90-day no-risk guarantee

price protection guarantee

full-year warranty

lifetime warranty

If you are not completely satisfied, just return it within _____ days and you'll owe nothing.

...we will promptly refund every penny.

If I am not completely satisfied, I will return it within _____ days for a full refund.

You must be completely satisfied or you pay nothing.

If for any reason you are not completely satisfied with your purchase, simply return it within _____ days and we'll refund the full amount.

I'll see that your money is promptly refunded.

If _____ isn't every bit as special as we say it is, simply return it to us within _____ days for a full refund.

This _____ is guaranteed to _____ or you can return it to us for a full refund.

We stand behind our _____ with a money-back guarantee.

We're so confident that you'll like _____, we're willing to back it up with a...

I personally guarantee it.

We guarantee that every item in this catalog is truthfully described. If for any reason you are not completely satisfied, ...

If you decide to return it, you'll be entitled to a prompt refund.

Your _____ is backed with a full-year warranty.

---

For further inspiration, see:

**Trial Offer/No Obligation**

**Persuading the Reader (Part 3)**

# Order Information

Here's how the program works:

Price includes:

Package includes:

Send for our colorful brochure.

☐ Yes, please enroll me...

☐ Yes, I accept your invitation to...

☐ Yes, I want to learn about...

☐ Yes, I want to enjoy...

Rush me the...

Please accept my order for...

Please ship _____ copies of...

Please send me the following items:

Indicate your choices on the list below.

Just mail the enclosed card...

Mail the enclosed card today!

To order your _____, simply fill out the coupon and mail it to...

Just reach for your phone...

Use our toll-free hotline...

I enclose $_____ in total payment.

☐ Payment enclosed.

☐ Please bill me.

☐ Please bill my __ (Visa, etc.)

Please make payment by check, money order, or credit card.

Charge it!

You will be billed in convenient monthly installments.

Your order will be filled promptly.

Your _____ will be on its way...

overnight shipping

Immediate delivery!

Please check the way your name and address appear on the label and make any corrections necessary.

For further inspiration, see:
**Making Contact (Part 3)**
**Sample Order Forms (Appendix)**

# PART 5
# SPECIAL STRATEGIES

Pulling Out All the Stops to Make Your Point

# Enhancing Your Company's Image

We've pledged to work harder than ever.

our total commitment to...

a labor of love

our dedication to...

our distinctive style of...

We believe in...

We investigate...

We search out...

We uncover...

We serve...

We uphold...

We honor...

We affirm...

We're dedicated to...

We take great pride in...

We're committed to...

We demand excellence...

We recognize the realities of...

We don't play games with...

Day after day, we...

We have served major multinational companies in the areas of...

Here are just a few of our clients:

What's our formula for success?

Despite what you may have heard, ...

We meet every challenge...

...has presented us with a unique challenge.

Are we claiming too much? We don't think so.

Who you buy from can be just as important as what you buy.

We're familiar with every nuance of...

We offer the added advantage of...

The key word is *quality*.

*You* are the one who benefits.

The leader in _____ for over _____ years.

The most trusted name in _____.

---

For further inspiration, see:
**Knocking the Competition**

**Heads and Slogans (Part 1)**
**Distinguished (Part 2)**
**Experienced/Expert (Part 2)**
**Honest (Part 2)**
**Improved (Part 2)**
**Reliable/Solid (Part 2)**
**Results (Part 2)**
**Service/Help (Part 2)**
**Superior (Part 2)**

# Justifying a High Price

_____ may cost more, but it's worth more.

intelligently priced at $_____

Why pay $_____ for a _____, when for a few dollars more, you could have a _____?

for people who can have whatever they want

for people with expensive tastes

because you're worth it

Living well is the best revenge.

Isn't it better to spend a little more now, instead of a lot more later?

You will be billed in monthly installments of just $_____.

Take a year to pay.

Your credit is good with us.

_____ will save you money in the long run.

Our rates may be higher, but we'll cut costs by getting the job done faster.

Isn't it worth paying a little extra for...?

Don't you deserve the best?

the Rolls-Royce of _____

flagrantly expensive

You probably thought you couldn't afford _____.

You're paying for quality.

Allow yourself a little luxury.

a luxury that's within reach

not as expensive as you think

Every distinguished home should have a _____.

For further inspiration, see:
**Luxurious (Part 2)**
**Status (Part 2)**
**Stylish (Part 2)**
**Superior (Part 2)**

# Knocking the Competition

Accept no substitutes.

Don't be taken in by...

Don't be seduced by...

Don't be deceived by...

Don't waste your hard-earned money on...

No other _____ comes close.

Our _____ has spawned a host of imitators.

pale imitations of...

pale replicas of...

clones

fly-by-night

less reputable

second-rate

cheap

no-name

_____ would have you believe that...

a maze of...

entangles you in...

No other _____ gives you...

Unlike other _____, ...

_____ is imitated but not equaled.

Don't fall for...

inflated claims made by...

If you're confused by the current deluge of...

We give you more _____ than any other _____.

_____% more _____ than our nearest rival

Nobody can match our prices.

Nobody beats _____.

can't match...

can't compare...

There's no comparison.

Don't settle for second best.

We're still number one.

---

For further inspiration, see:
**Enhancing Your Company's Image**

**Authentic (Part 2)**
**Distinguished (Part 2)**
**Reliable/Solid (Part 2)**
**Superior (Part 2)**

# Using Demographics to Impress

What kind of people use (choose, read, buy) _____?

upscale people

serious people

people who play as hard as they work

professional/managerial

upwardly mobile

educated

bright

intelligent

curious

young

successful

aware

active

affluent

$50,000+ HHI (household income)

young spenders

young achievers

_____% are between 25 and 44

_____% hold professional/managerial jobs

_____% own their own homes

_____% earn over $30,000

_____% attended college

the cream of the crop

the creme de la creme

a highly selective group

key decision makers

a most attractive audience

involved adult readers

buying power

impulsive buyers

They're a $_____ market.

If you want to score with people like that, ...

---

For further inspiration, see:
**Status (Part 2)**
**Superior (Part 2)**

# Flattering the Reader

You have been highly recommended to us.

We extend this invitation to a special few.

You demand the best.

You're the toughest critic we know.

You are among the first to receive this special offer.

You're an active member of your community.

You're very selective when it comes to _____.

You're the kind of person who…

You're going places.

You strive for excellence.

Your _____ says a lot about you.

You chart your own course.

You set uncommon goals for yourself.

We know that you…

for people with high standards

for special people

for men and women of distinction

for those who appreciate the finest

for intelligent, influential individuals like you

your discerning taste in _____

a tribute to your taste

_____ celebrates the kind of excellence exemplified by people like you.

This _____ is being sent only to those who fully appreciate…

achievers

doers

thoughtful, literate people

leaders

---

For further inspiration, see:
**Status (Part 2)**

# Appealing for Contributions

Please give...

Please try to give *something*.

I hope you will join in contributing...

Your financial support is needed.

We desperately need your help.

We cannot continue our work without your help.

We rely entirely on the generosity of friends like you.

Won't you please help?

The future of _____ lies in your hands.

This is your chance to help...

With your help, we can go on...

_____ needs your support.

Your gift can help _____ survive.

You can make the difference.

Your contribution will help feed...

Their future depends on you.

Your generosity can give them a new lease on life.

a future filled with hope and promise

Without your help, all the gains of the last few years could evaporate.

Be a patron of the arts.

This is your chance to help our nation (party, city, etc.) meet the challenges of the coming years.

volunteer

support

contribute

donate

your philanthropy

a benevolent gesture

charity

Help save...

Help us reach our goal.

Give anything you can.

As a result of recent federal cutbacks, we need your support more than ever.

In return, you'll gain the satisfaction of...

I know you won't let us down.

You'll help assure the future of...

Your gift is tax-deductible.

Your help makes a critical difference.

---

For further inspiration, see:
**Flattering the Reader**

# Following Through

Thank you for writing us...

Thank you for your inquiry.

Thank you for your interest in...

Here is the information you asked for.

We are pleased to learn of your interest
in...

You couldn't have picked a better time to
ask us about...

Recently we sent you literature on...

The _____ you asked for has been sent to
you...

You are to be commended for your
interest in...

I'm glad you sent for the information
on _____. When you learn the facts, I
think you'll be glad, too.

For further inspiration, see:
**Making Contact (Part 3)**

# APPENDIX

# Categories of Copy

CATALOGS introduce your company's entire product line, or a preselected portion of the product line, in the form of a booklet with entries on each product. Copy should be kept brief, crisp, to the point; the reader must have instant access to key facts. Lead off your entries with powerful adjectives and verbs; avoid beginning with a flat "This _____ is..." Sentence fragments are perfectly acceptable—almost mandatory. Products can be grouped by category, price range, or any of a number of other systems. The only rule about grouping is to be consistent throughout. It's generally a good idea to display associated products together on a single page or spread; that way you'll encourage multiple purchases. You may want to add an upbeat introductory message about your company; a friendly exhortation from the president is almost always effective. The order form should be bound in, easy to understand, and easily detached.

BROCHURES are folded, glossy-looking pieces that focus on a more limited range of products. Your copy should unfold strategically in persuasive, full-bodied prose. Break up the copy into easily managed units with catchy subheads. Outstanding product features can be highlighted with "bullets" (prominent dots before each point) or other visual attention-getters. The ideal order form is a separate return-response card, but a clip-out order coupon will do the job if you want to cut costs.

SALES LETTERS can be your most effective selling tool—personal and persuasive like a one-on-one sales pitch, yet without the intense pressure that can force a customer to keep his guard up. Sales letters have exhibited a lamentable tendency to run on at great length—six or eight pages is no longer uncommon—but such voluminous epistles can only tax a reader's patience. Better to drive home your point within a page or two. If you want, you can vary the paragraph widths (as do most direct-mail copywriters) as a visual gimmick to hold the reader's attention. Adopt a natural, unstilted writing style that follows everyday speech patterns: no *as per*'s, *herein*'s, or *please find enclosed*'s. You don't even have to begin with a salutation. A catchy headline across the top of the page will grab the reader's attention.

SPACE ADS are simply the printed ads that fill most newspapers and magazines. They are as various as breeds of dogs—from the sleek wolfhounds of Madison Avenue to the plucky mutts that yelp for attention in the back pages of men's magazines. However divergent their styles, successful space ads all share a few key traits: they grab the reader within two or three seconds, they know their audience, and they convey a potent message within the confines of their allotted space.

Today's slick space ads tend to consist of short sentences and sentence fragments, almost conversational in tone, yet somewhat tight and reserved. I would suggest that you study these ads in your favorite magazine, then decide whether you want to emulate them or ignore them.

COMMERCIALS are space ads broadcast over the airwaves. Unlike other forms of advertising, commercials give you the advantage of a captive audience. You're free to use humor if it suits your purpose (when was the last time you read a funny brochure?) and you can even write the words to jingles if you're so inclined. Keep in mind that a well-written commercial follows the natural patterns of human speech; it pays to have a colleague read the copy aloud before you submit it.

PRESS RELEASES or NEWS RELEASES announce your message to the news media, which in turn will (you hope) disseminate it to the public. A good press release is "newsy" above all else; the editor who reads it is looking for material that will make a lively story. Get attention with a powerful headline and a banner that reads "For immediate release" (or something equally urgent). Wildly enthusiastic press releases without editorial substance are disparagingly referred to as "puffery" by the seasoned pros. And puffery invariably ends up in the waste basket.

STATEMENT STUFFERS are minibrochures enclosed with invoices and other billing statements. Limited by their diminutive dimensions (and by the tend-

ency of the recipient to chuck them away unread), stuffers must *shout* to be heard. Use a dynamic "grabber" and crisp catalog-style copy with a simple order form on the reverse side.

POSTERS and POINT-OF-PURCHASE DISPLAYS are simply "grabbers" displayed in stores to catch the consumer's attention and motivate impulse buying. Remember that your display will be competing against dozens of other units in a vast battleground of products. See the section "Grabbers" for ideas.

# Puffspeak—And Its Alternative

What follows is a partial listing of inflated words and phrases that have pummeled their way into our language over the objections of writers and other worthy citizens. Some of these terms are elaborate disguises for mundane or unpalatable concepts; others are simply poor usage. Those I've marked with an asterisk can be safely (even effectively) put to use in your copywriting, but try to assess your audience first.

| Puffspeak | Translation |
|---|---|
| access (used as a verb)* | obtain |
| at this point in time | now |
| Byzantine | scheming, elaborately contrived |
| cash flow* | income |
| conceptualize | think |
| continuum | link |
| cost-effective | profitable, money-saving |
| counterproductive* | futile |
| crisis situation | crisis |
| effectuate | bring about |
| enclosed herewith | inside |
| feedback* | response |
| finalize | finish |
| human resources | personnel |
| impact (used as a verb) | affect |
| impact negatively | worsen |
| infrastructure | facilities |
| inoperative | doesn't work |
| interface (used as a verb) | meet, work with |

| Puffspeak | Translation |
|---|---|
| literally (as in "literally rolling in the aisles") | virtually, practically |
| macro-anything | big |
| mainstreaming | rejoining |
| mega-anything* | big |
| meta-anything | (too vague to define, usually implies transcendence, going "beyond") |
| methodology | rules |
| modality | style |
| module | part, unit |
| networking | making connections |
| normalize | return to normal, stabilize |
| operational | working |
| optimal* | ideal |
| optimize | improve |
| overriding | major |
| parameters | limits, guidelines |
| para-anything | (see "meta-anything") |
| parenting | raising children |
| parity | equality |
| prioritize | rank in order of importance |
| pursuant to | according to |
| ramifications* | consequences |
| scenario | sequence of events |

| Puffspeak | Translation |
|---|---|
| schizophrenic (as in "a schizophrenic foreign policy") | two-faced, conflicting |
| shortfall | loss of income |
| state-of-the-art* | latest, most advanced |
| stonewalling | lying |
| systematize | organize |
| target (used as a verb) | plan, schedule |
| terminated | finished, fired |
| thrust (used as a noun) | intent |
| time frame | schedule |
| track record* | achievements |
| upwardly mobile* | successful, affluent |
| viable | workable |
| What's the bottom line?* | How do I benefit? |

# Wordy Expressions

On this list are some prime examples of phrases that amount to little more than "dead wood." Most can be trimmed to a single word.

| Avoid | Replace It With |
| --- | --- |
| at the present time | now |
| at this point in time | now |
| as of this date | now |
| at that time | then |
| at that point in time | then |
| during the time that | when, during |
| at which time | when, during |
| on the occasion of | when, during |
| subsequent to | after |
| on the grounds that | because |
| as a result of | because |
| owing to the fact that | because |
| accounted for by the fact that | because |
| by virtue of the fact that | because |
| in spite of the fact that | although |
| with reference to | about |
| pertaining to | about |
| in the event that | if |
| whether or not | whether |
| the question as to whether | whether |
| at an early date | soon |
| be in receipt of | get |

| Avoid | Replace It With |
|---|---|
| owing to the fact that | since |
| come in contact with | meet |
| during the time that | while |
| come to a decision as to | decide |
| reach a conclusion as to | decide |
| make use of | use |
| be cognizant of | know |
| exhibit a tendency to | tend to |
| give consideration to | consider |
| in close proximity | near |
| it is often the case that | often |
| make an examination of | examine |
| make mention of | mention |
| he is a man who | he |
| this is a subject that | this subject |
| after very careful consideration | after considering |
| is of the opinion | believes |
| make inquiry regarding | inquire |

# Commonly Misspelled Words

Nothing can subvert the cause of good copy like a well-placed spelling error; the surprising thing is that so many everyday words are fraught with opportunities for mistakes. This list, based on American spelling conventions, should help you catch many potential errors before they find their way into print.

*Note:* Parentheses indicate acceptable alternate spellings. In general, the shorter spellings are preferred; e.g., *canceled* takes preference over *cancelled*.

aberration
abridg(e)ment
absence
accede
accelerate
acceptable
accessible
accessory
accommodate
accumulate
achieve
acknowledg(e)ment
acquainted
acquiesce
acquire
acrylic
aerial
aesthetically (esthetically)
ag(e)ing
aggressive
alcohol
allege
allotted
all right
already
ambience (-ance)
analogous
analysis
anonymous

apparatus
archetype
associate
athlete
attendance
awkward

balloon
bazaar
beggar
believe
benefit(t)ed
biased
bouillon
breathe
bulletin
burglar

caffeine
calendar
campaign
cancel(l)ed
cancellation
candor
cannot
caricature
casualty
catalog(ue)
category
cemetery

changeable
channel(l)ed
character
chief
choose
cigarette
circuit
clientele
climactic
collaborate
colleague
colossal
column
commemorate
commission
committee
compel
competent
conceive
conjure
connoisseur
conscience
conscientious
consensus
consistency
contemporary
coolly
copywriter
correspondence
counsel(l)ed
counterfeit
courteous

deceive
deductible
defense
dependent

despair
desperate
deterrent
develop
development
diagram(m)ed
diagrammatic
dialog(ue)
dilemma
disappear
disappoint
disastrous
disciplined
disillusioned
dissension
disservice
dissolve
distributor

ecstasy
edgewise
eerie
eighth
elegant
embarrass
enclosure
encumbrance
endeavor
endorsement
entrepreneur
exaggerate
exceed
excusable
exercise
exhibitor
exhilarating
existence

exorbitant
extraordinary
exuberant

feasible
fiery
flammable
flier
fluorescent
focus(s)ed
foresee
foreword (preface)
forgettable
forty
forward (ahead)
fulfill (-fil)
fulfilled

gaiety
genealogy
grammar
grievous
guarantee

handkerchief
harass
height
heroes
hindrance
homeward
homogeneous
hors d'oeuvre(s)
hungrily
hygiene
hypocrisy

illegible
imperil(l)ed
independent

indict
indispensable
ingenious
innocuous
innuendo
inoculate
installed
instilled
intention
iridescent
irrelevant
irreparable
irresistible

judg(e)ment

keenness
knowledgeable

label(l)ed
laboratory
laid
leisure
lengthwise
level(l)ed
liable
liaison
license
lik(e)able
likely
liqueur (cordial)
liquor
loathsome

madam
maintenance
maneuver
marvel(l)ous

mathematics
matinee
meager (-re)
medicine
medi(a)eval
memento(e)s
mileage
milieu
miniature
minuscule (miniscule)
miscellaneous
mischievous
misspell
model(l)ed
monogrammed
mortgage
movable

naive
necessary
negligent
nonplussed (-plused)
nuisance

occasionally
occurrence
offense
omelet(te)
omission
oneself
onward
optimism

paid
panel(l)ed
parallel
paralyzed
paraphernalia
partisan

pastime
pavilion
perennial
permanent
permissible
perseverance
personnel
picnicking
plaque
plausible
playwright
possession
potato
potatoes
practice
precede
predecessor
predictable
preferred
presence
pretense
privilege
procedure
proceed
pronunciation
propeller

quarrel(l)ing
questionnaire

rarity
receipt
receive
recommend
reconnaissance
registrar
reinforce
reminiscence

remittance
renaissance
reparable
repellent (-ant)
resistance
resource
restaurant
restaura(n)teur
rhyme
rhythm
rival(l)ed

sacrilegious
salable
satellite
scenery
scissors
secretary
seize
separate
serviceable
shovel(l)ed
silhouette
sincerely
skeptic
smo(u)lder
software
souvenir
specimen
strategy
stubbornness
subtlety
successful
summarize
supersede
surreptitious
synonymous
systematic

terrific
theater (-re)
threshold
tomato
tomatoes
total(l)ed
tranquillity (-lity)
transferable
tries
truly
twelfth
tying

vacillate
vacuum
valuable
vegetable
vehicle
vengeance
veteran
veterinarian
vicious

warehouse
warranty
weird
wholly
whims(e)y
willful (wilful)
wily
withhold
wool(l)en

yacht
yield
yoke (coupling)
yolk (egg)

zany
zigzag

# Commonly Confused Words

Our language is filled with deceptive word-pairs that seem to exist only to trip up unsuspecting writers. Don't be fooled by outward appearances of similarity. As you'll see on this list, totally unrelated concepts can be cloaked in nearly identical words.

**accede**—to agree
**exceed**—to surpass

**accept**—to receive
**except**—excluding

**adapt**—to adjust to
**adopt**—to accept formally
    or take as one's own

**affect**—(v) to influence
**effect**—(v) to bring about, (n) result

**aid**—help
**aide**—staff member

**all ready**—prepared
**already**—previously

**allusion**—reference to
**illusion**—false image
**delusion**—false belief

**among**—more than two involved
**between**—two involved

**ascent**—rise
**assent**—consent

**beside**—alongside
**besides**—also

**climactic**—pertaining to a climax
**climatic**—pertaining to climate

**complement**—complete
**compliment**—praise

**continual**—repeated
**continuous**—uninterrupted

**council**—(n) a group
**counsel**—(n) advice, (v) to advise

**disinterested**—impartial
**uninterested**—apathetic

**elicit**—to draw out
**illicit**—illegal

**eminent**—prominent
**imminent**—in the immediate future

**fewer**—numbers
**less**—amount

**flaunt**—to show off
**flout**—to defy

**imply**—to suggest
**infer**—to draw a conclusion

**it's**—contraction for *it is*
**its**—possessive

**loose**—unattached
**lose**—to suffer loss

**perquisite**—privilege
**prerequisite**—requirement

**precede**—to go before
**proceed**—to begin or continue

**presently**—soon
**at present**—now

**principal**—chief
**principle** —rule

**sight**—something seen
**site**—place

**stationary**—fixed
**stationery**—writing supplies

**their**—possessive
**there**—adverb, showing location
**they're**—contraction of *they are*

**who's**—contraction of *who is*
**whose**—possessive

**you're**—contraction of *you are*
**your**—possessive

# Selling Yourself

## Personal Qualities

These words represent personality traits people in the business world find positive and attractive. Review this list and select the words that seem to describe *you*. Plan to use them (with moderation, of course) in your resume, cover letters, and interviews.

able
accurate
adaptable
adept
adroit
aggressive
alert
ambitious
analytical
articulate
attractive

bilingual
bright

capable
competent
confident
consistent
cooperative
creative

dedicated
dependable
detail-oriented
dynamic

educated
effective
efficient
energetic
enthusiastic
executive caliber

experienced
expert
extraverted

fast
fit
flexible
formidable
friendly

gregarious

hardworking
healthy
highly motivated
honest

imaginative
ingenious
innovative
intelligent
inventive
Ivy League

judicious

licensed
literate

managerial
motivated
multilingual
multitalented

nonsmoking

organized
outgoing
outstanding

patient
people-oriented
perceptive
personable
poised
polished
principled
productive
professional
proficient

qualified
quick-thinking

ready
reliable
resourceful
responsible
robust

sane
scholarly
scrupulous
seasoned
self-assured

self-reliant
serious
shrewd
skilled
smart
spirited
stable
successful

talented
tenacious
top-level
trained
trustworthy

upbeat

valuable
versatile
veteran

well-educated
well-groomed
willing
witty
worldly

young
youthful

## "Action" Verbs

These words make a strong impression when you want to promote your achievements. They're ideal for resumes, cover letters, reports and memos.

accelerated
accessed
achieved
acquired

acted
administered
advised
appointed

arranged
assigned
assisted
attended

booked
broadened
budgeted

checked
collaborated
competed
completed
conceived
conducted
constructed
consulted
contributed
controlled
coordinated
correlated
counseled
created

delegated
demonstrated
designed
determined
developed
devised
directed
doubled

edited
effected
eliminated
established
evaluated
executed
expanded

expedited
explored

formulated
founded

generated
guided

handled
headed
helped
hired

identified
implemented
improved
increased
initiated
instituted
instructed
interacted
introduced
invented
investigated

launched
led

maintained
managed
marketed
met with
monitored
motivated

negotiated

opened
operated
organized
oversaw

participated
performed
pinpointed
planned
prepared
presented
prevented
processed
produced
programmed
promoted
proposed
provided
purchased

recruited
reduced
reorganized
reported
represented
resolved
restructured
reversed
revised

saved
scheduled
secured
selected
set priorities
set up
shaped
sold
solved
structured
supervised

taught
tested
tightened
trained
trimmed

upgraded
utilized

won
worked with
wrote

# Sample Order Forms

**Business-to-Business**

## ORDER FORM

T.J. Eckleberg Optical Co., Inc.
1919 Wilson Blvd.
Flushing, N.Y. 11355

Please ship the following items:

| Item No. | Product Description | Quantity | Price |
|---|---|---|---|
|  |  |  |  |
|  |  |  |  |
|  |  |  |  |
|  | Total |  |  |

**Dealers:** See Universal Optics Handbook for discount schedule.

**Terms:** 2/10 EOM net 30 days. All sales FOB Flushing, N.Y. Postage and handling are prepaid and added to invoice. If order amounts to $50.00 or less after applicable discount, please enclose check or money order including 10% ($2.00 minimum) to cover postage and handling.

**New Accounts:** Order must total $100.00 or more after applicable discount to qualify for purchasing on open account. All orders under $100.00 must be prepaid.

**Schools and Institutions:** 25% discount on all orders: To qualify, please use official purchase order. Postage and handling are prepaid and added to invoice.

## SATISFACTION GUARANTEED ON ALL ORDERS.

For immediate service, contact your local rep or call our toll-free number: 800-001-1894. In New York call (212) 101-2933.

*(continued)*

**Please Print**

Account Number _____ Sales Rep _____

Order Number _____ Date _____

Shipping Instructions:   ☐ Parc. Post   ☐ UPS   ☐ Special Del.   ☐ Spec. Hand.

☐ Other _____

**Bill To:**

Name _____

Address _____

City _____

State _____ Zip _____

Prices subject to change without notice.

**Ship To:**

Name _____

Address _____

City _____

State _____ Zip _____

# Consumer (Catalog Order Form)

## Mail Your Order To:

Dr. Organix Natural Products
One Greenway Drive
Piscataway, N.J. 08854

Affix address label here.
Please make any corrections
in the space provided below.

### Bill to:

Name _____

Address _____

City _____

State _____ Zip _____

For instant service, call (201) 999-0009
between 9 a.m. and 5 p.m. Eastern time.

### Ship to (other than yourself):

Name _____

Address _____

City _____

State _____ Zip _____

Item No. _____

☐ Enclose gift card

Please select the items you want:

| Item No. | Title/Description | How many | $ Amount |
|----------|-------------------|----------|----------|
|          |                   |          |          |
|          |                   |          |          |
|          |                   |          |          |
|          |                   |          |          |
| **Total** | | | |
| Shipping | | | |
| Sales Tax (N.J. Residents) | | | |
| **Total of Above** | | | |

*(continued)*

_____

_____

Please make payment by check, money order, or credit card.
($10.00 minimum charge order)

☐ Payment enclosed.                    Please bill my: ☐ Visa

☐ Master Card

☐ American Express

Acct. No. _____ Exp. Date _____

Signature _____

## SATISFACTION GUARANTEED!

Every item in this catalog is truthfully described.

If for any reason you are not completely satisfied with your purchase, simply return it to us within 15 days and we'll promptly refund the full amount!

Please detach here and insert in envelope.
Make sure that you enclose your payment or credit card information.

Thank you for your order.

# Further Reading

## Copywriting Texts

Burton, Philip W. *Advertising Copywriting.* New York: McGraw-Hill, 1983.

Hafer, W. Keith and Gordon E. White. *Advertising Writing.* St. Paul, Minnesota: West Publishing Co., 1982.

Malickson, David L. and John W. Nason. *Advertising: How to Write the Kind That Works.* New York: Scribner's, 1982.

Milton, Shirley F. and Arthur A. Winters. *The Creative Connection: Advertising Copy and Idea Visualization.* New York: Fairchild, 1981.

Norins, Hanley. *The Compleat Copywriter. A Comprehensive Guide to All Phases of Advertising Communication.* Melbourne, Florida: Krieger, 1980.

Parker, Robert B. *Mature Advertising: A Handbook of Effective Advertising Copy.* Reading, Massachusetts: Addison-Wesley, 1981.

Schwab, V. *How to Write Advertisements.* Belfast, Maine: Porter, 1981.

Schwab, Victor O. *How to Write a Good Advertisement.* North Hollywood, California: Wilshire, 1980.

## Other Valuable Titles for People Who Write Copy

Bates, Jefferson D. *Writing with Precision.* Washington: Acropolis Books, 1980. Includes a usage handbook along with tips on avoiding "gobbledygook" in writing.

Bly, Robert W. and Gary Blake. *Technical Writing: Structure, Standards and Style.* New York: McGraw-Hill, 1982. A compact but reasonably comprehensive style guide.

Fielden, John S., Jean D. Fielden and Ronald E. Dulek. *The Business Writing Style Book.* Englewood Cliffs, New Jersey: Prentice-Hall, 1984. How to set the right tone in your business communication.

Geffner, Andrea B. *Business English.* Woodbury, New York: Barron's, 1982. Notable for its concise, straightforward writing techniques and abundant supply of model letters, the latter representing virtually every type of business correspondence.

Powers, Melvin. *How to Get Rich in Mail Order.* North Hollywood, California: Wilshire, 1980. A wild romp through the "I Made a Million Dollars in Two Weeks" school of copywriting. Packed with supremely tasteless (and superbly effective) examples of now-classic ads, this hefty tome is a "must-read" for anyone involved in direct mail.

Smith, Cynthia. *How to Get Big Results from a Small Advertising Budget.* New York. Hawthorn Books, 1973. Aimed at the entrepreneur of a small company; covers the gamut from copy to public relations.

Stansfield, Richard H. *The Dartnell Advertising Manager's Handbook.* Chicago: Dartnell Corp., 1969. The most solid reference book of its kind—over 1500 pages with an emphasis on industrial advertising, including a couple of good chapters on copywriting.

Strunk, William and E.B. White. *The Elements of Style.* New York: Macmillan, 1979 (revision of earlier editions). Slim, ageless guide to English usage, composition and the nuances of style. E.B. White, of *New Yorker* fame, is one of the century's leading apostles of pure, understated prose.

Wademan, Victor. *Money-Making Advertising.* New York: John Wiley and Sons, 1981. A useful informal text.

Zinsser, William. *On Writing Well.* New York: Harper & Row, 1980. A solid guide to nonfiction writing techniques; another worthwhile addition to the writer's personal library.

# Key Word Index

*Titles of topics are printed in boldface type*

# About the Author

Richard Bayan currently holds the position of Copy Chief at Day-Timers. For seven years, he served as Chief Copywriter at Barron's Educational Series. A former staff writer for Time-Life Books, he first broke into print with a series of essays in *National Review* and later joined the staff of *The New American Review*. Mr. Bayan graduated from Rutgers with a major in history, then earned a master's degree in journalism from the University of Illinois.